Thomas Jefferson

by Pat McCarthy

Editorial Offices: Glenview, Illinois • Parsippany, New Jersey • New York, New York

Sales Offices: Needham, Massachusetts • Duluth, Georgia • Glenview, Illinois
Coppell, Texas • Sacramento, California • Mesa, Arizona

Thomas Jefferson

Jefferson Had Good Ideas

Thomas Jefferson had many ideas. He was good at writing his ideas down. His ideas helped form our government.

Jefferson was born April 13, 1743, in Virginia. Virginia was a colony then. It belonged to England. England had thirteen American colonies at that time.

Jefferson Goes to School

Jefferson went to a one-room school. He learned to read, write, and do math. He learned French, Latin, and Greek. Jefferson went to college in Virginia at the age of sixteen.

The College of William and Mary in Virginia

Jefferson studied law.

Jefferson later studied law with a famous lawyer named George Wythe. The two men became friends and stayed friends all their lives.

Jefferson Is Elected to Office

Jefferson became a lawyer. He did not like the way England ruled the colonies.

Jefferson married Martha Skelton. He built a house called Monticello.

Some people in the colonies were unhappy with the way the British were ruling them.

Jefferson wrote that England should not make laws for the colonies. People in the colonies wanted to have a **direct democracy.**

Jefferson's home, Monticello

The Colonies Say They Are Free

People from many colonies met in Philadelphia in 1774. This **council** was called the First Continental Congress.

The next year, the Second Continental Congress said that England could no longer rule them. They chose Jefferson to write a paper saying the colonies were free. They called this paper the Declaration of Independence. Jefferson said it told what Americans were thinking.

Preamble to the Declaration of Independence

Signing of the Declaration of Independence

The Colonies Fight a War

The colonies fought a war to get free from England. It was called the Revolutionary War. It took eight years to win this war.

Jefferson wrote an important paper about religion. It said people could worship in their own way.

Jefferson was elected **governor** of Virginia. Jefferson had a lot of **responsibility**. He needed to save Virginia from the British. He did not have enough money or supplies for the soldiers.

Jefferson Goes Home

Jefferson went back home after being governor. He wrote a book about Virginia. The war ended in 1781.

The next year Jefferson's wife died. He was very sad and stayed in his room for three weeks.

Jefferson wrote many important things.

Jefferson Serves His Country

Jefferson was later elected to Congress. He wrote many important papers.

Jefferson went to France to help make treaties, or agreements, with other countries. He worked with John Adams and Benjamin Franklin. Jefferson stayed in France for five years.

John Adams

George Washington was elected the first President of the United States. Jefferson was Washington's Secretary of State. He helped the country get along with other countries.

When John Adams was President, Jefferson was Vice President. Jefferson and Adams had very different ideas.

Jefferson as President

Later, Jefferson was elected the third President of the United States. He worked hard.

Thomas Jefferson

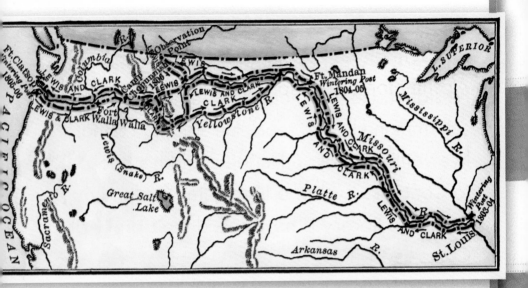

Lewis and Clark explored the new land.

In 1803 the United States bought a very large piece of land called Louisiana from France. Jefferson sent Meriwether Lewis and William Clark to explore the land. Lewis and Clark drew maps of the land and wrote in journals. Many people moved west to settle on the new land.

After Jefferson Was President

Jefferson went back to Monticello after being President. He was happy to be home.

Jefferson liked to read. He said, "I cannot live without books." He later sold his books to Congress to start a library in Washington, D.C. This library is now called the Library of Congress.

Library of Congress

Jefferson invented the turning bookstand.

Jefferson liked to invent things. He invented a desk he could carry with him. He also invented a machine to make macaroni.

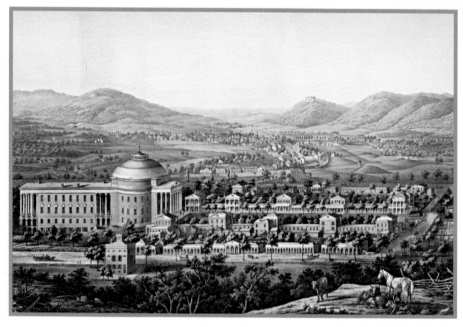

University of Virginia

Jefferson started the University of Virginia. He invited all the students to dinner at his house.

Thomas Jefferson Dies

Thomas Jefferson died on July 4, 1826. It was fifty years from the day the Declaration of Independence was signed. He was eighty-three years old.

Jefferson is buried at Monticello. He planned his own tombstone. It says:

HERE WAS BURIED

THOMAS JEFFERSON

AUTHOR OF THE

DECLARATION

OF

AMERICAN INDEPENDENCE

OF THE

STATUTE OF VIRGINIA

FOR

RELIGIOUS FREEDOM

AND FATHER OF THE

UNIVERSITY OF VIRGINIA

Glossary

council a group of people who make laws and rules for a community

direct democracy government run by the people who live under it

governor a person elected as the head of a state in the United States

responsibility a duty; something that must be done